Slip through the Keyhole

Slip through the Keyhole

ADRIA ESTRIBOU

WingSound Media

Slip through the Keyhole
First Edition (2016). Published in the United States.

Published by Wing Sound Media LLC
www.WingSoundMedia.com
info@wingsoundmedia.com
PO Box 3371
Honolulu, HI 96801

Cover illustrations by Petricia Suprapto
http://jambalroti.deviantart.com/

Interior illustrations by Nguyen Kim Hoang Nhu (KimZ)
www.kimzillu.com

Poetry, American—21st Century
Lyric poetry
Love poetry
Contemplation
Mysticism
Mystical union

ISBN for second printing:
978-1-967025-03-9

for the Revealer

Contents

Seeds   1

How does the thread   3
The seed already contains   5
I asked the tree   7
"I want" is a closed fist   9
The mind whispers secrets   11
The little plants take more water   13
How can I perceive   15
Let us not be curious   17
Learn from a Rat   19
Love cannot be defined, confined or broken   21
To find happiness we seek   23

One   25

Love is not in one leaf   27
Many beings have walked with me   29
It is only too hard   31
Outside the egg   33
Death   35
We don't feel   37
You made us two   39

Hide & Seek   41

The tracing of a coin   43
Take from love "I want"   45

I see you in a thousand puppets   47

Clouds above the Water   49

The moon plays push-me—pull-you   51

All identities are false   53

I catch the tear drops   55

Dancing has no contradiction   57

Don't wilt from loneliness   59

Like breath and lung   61

You stopped the game of hide and seek   63

Q & A   65

What should I bring you?   67

What is God's address?   69

Why doesn't God wear a watch?   71

In the darkness   73

Which is better   75

These five horses   77

Will I always love you?   79

Empty   81

This world has taught me   83

I have a pile of concepts for sale   85

My Master is so greedy   87

Darkness flees before light   89

Glass Half Full   91

The world says fill up   93

Empty of thoughts   95

My atoms 97

You told me to leave 99

It is not bravery to battle 101

On the dance floor 103

NOW is too tiny to fit identities 105

Line by line the ink runs from the pages 107

In the school of the Beloved 109

I saw you 111

Flight 113

The door to the Beloved 115

When I saw a bird's nest 117

The ego cries 119

In the moment of leaping 121

The Choice 123

If there are one or one thousand 125

Sweep me up in your infinity 127

I am feasting on Love 129

I sleep so that you can wake me 131

I walk the hallways of my childhood 133

I had to break the vase of love 135

Somewhere between 137

Dizzy 139

The touch of the Lover 141

About the Author 143

Seeds

How does the thread
merge with the dress?

How does the drop
merge with the ocean?

How does the pattern
merge with the butterfly wing?

How does the air
merge with the sky?

How does the grape
merge with the vine?

How does the soul
merge with the Divine?

The seed already contains
the full flowering of
the tree

I already contain
the absence
of me

I asked the tree:
No fruit
Not much shade
What use are you?

The tree said:
Utility is a false hope
Once you accomplish
What then?

"I want" is a closed fist
Nothing can get in

Letting go is an open palm
that holds the whole world

A farmer must let go of the seeds in her hands
for them to fall onto fertile soil

The mind whispers secrets:
it knows, it knows the way

The ego fights for Mine

I'd rather be a puppet of the Divine

The little plants take more water,
the gardener said
The big trees have deep roots to store the rain

Break out of the pot you're in
Root deep into the source of all things

How can I perceive
the One beyond perception?

I can't find the tools I need
in the illusion factory

Let us not be curious about
the endless colors of the dream
Let us be curious, instead, about the dreamer

Let us not strive to preserve, possess,
keep, hold on to, lock up
Instead let us see what can be opened wide

Let us not obsess about blood, phlegm and bone
Let us marvel at what brings the flesh sack to life

And what is this light?
that pierces through all veils and delusions
beckoning, beckoning, beckoning . . .

Learn from a Rat

I'm not learning as much as the rat in the maze
I keep pushing the same button, expecting more

Love is through the other door

Love cannot be defined, confined or broken
Love is alone

To perceive, we are many beings
To misperceive, we wear a body suit with senses
This is what makes the game

To find happiness we seek:
~ a marriage of conditional love
~ castles built on quicksand
~ to win a war against some "other"
~ to escape the crocodile of death

We chase these trinkets
around the merry-go-round
thinking we are getting so far ahead

Uncommon is the one who seeks:
~ bliss without opposite
~ flight without fall
~ Love without two

One

Love is not in one leaf
It is in every leaf
Not in one sunset
In every grain of sand

In every particle of air pulsing
In the wind's embrace
In the earth holding your footsteps
Lighting your way

Many beings have walked with me
~two-foot, four-foot friends~
I don't get to keep any of them

Many, many possessions
have passed through these hands
~beautiful, simple, expensive, flawed~
Not one possession will I leave this earth with

Many identities have formed over time
~child, lover, friend, businessperson, writer~
In the end, I don't get to keep any of them

Many thoughts have rolled through
~ideas, complaints, explanations, wonderments~
I can't keep even one

Many colors of emotions have come to visit
~rage, adoration, happiness, fear~
I can't hold on to any of them

In a world of change
only One is unchanging
and even that One
can't keep me

Because there are not two

It is only too hard
through the human view:
something to do
something to accomplish

But everything done and undone
is part of the One
You have always been what you seek

Outside the egg,
I am as tall as the sky
as small as a seed

All that you are
is within
and without of me

I've invested so much in separation
What wealth is left should never be spent there

Death

Nothing inside
Nothing outside

When the bottle breaks
nothing and nothing become One

We don't feel
the soft-gloved touch of time
but we see its mark

We think death is something
that only happens to others
or at 102

Why this ruckus over changing clothes?

Your costume fades, gets wrinkled
Remember you'll get to trade it in
for a whole new identity

The real trick is to stop
churning in the dyeing vat of rebirth
and live naked
as One

You made us two
so that I could adore you

All these vines
come from one root

Hide
&
Seek

The tracing of a coin
might look the same
but it won't buy even a trinket

This so called "love" (if you ___ I will love you)
is a merchant's game
It is a currency of zeros

We need another name for this Love:
Love without walls
Love without reason
Love without object
Love without season

The reflection will never become what it reflects
When we seek our Love in love
we only crack our head against the mirror glass

But it is a clue

Love is showing you itself in full splendor
You are the reflecting pool

Take from love "I want"
Take from love "I need"
Take from love its object
Take from love "I grieve"

Take from love "hold on"
Take from love "please, please"

What is left
this naked love
is the outer glow
of God's great Light

It is a passing glance in the mirror
reminding you who you are

I see you in a thousand puppets
I see you in the door

Each time you open up the curtains
all I can say is "more"

<u>Clouds above the Water</u>

A reflection is not real
But neither is the form it is reflecting

The sky is full of clouds tonight
but I know the stars still shine

I won't be fooled into thinking I'm not the One
because of the illusion of separation

The moon plays push-me—pull-you
with the tides
our emotions
our cycles
our dreams
the mood of night

The unchanging sun
as constant as breath
or the heart of God
daily showers us with life
sustenance
warmth
hope

Yet we write poems
about the hide-and-seek moon
and ignore the faithful sun
the source of the moon's light

The changing, fickle, desire-full moon
The blazing, content, illuminating sun

Will you live in reflection?
Or Light?

All identities are false

Not just the ones it would be convenient
to get rid of:
victim
child
wounded
"I"

But also
body
friend
disciple

Even the most precious
lover
and Beloved

All identities are false
They dance the lie of separation

I catch the tear drops
I see why you cry
looking in all the wrong places

Don't look outside
look within
Turn the right way 'round

Don't look for sunbeams in the moon
Stop running towards what can't be found

Do you want dross
or gold?
Before this stale life turns old
turn the right way 'round

If you water plastic flowers
they still won't grow
Turn the right way 'round

When you finally see
what you already are
tears will spring from joy

Dancing has no contradiction
unless it is standing still

Love has no contradiction
unless it is not arriving

Joy has no contradiction
unless it is creating walls

God has no contradiction
unless it is "my name is _____"

Transformation has no contradiction
unless it is holding on

Meditation has no contradiction
unless it is getting it right

Consciousness has no contradiction
unless it is choosing sleep

Master has no contradiction
unless it is closing the window

Let's pretend
to be separate fragments in the mirror
so we can dance

Don't wilt from loneliness
when you're made up of Love

Don't die of dehydration
while you're swimming in a lake

Drink!

Like breath and lung
we never meet
Yet I am animated by you

You are the fire in an unlit candle
the sound in the unstruck bell
the love with no object in the heart of man

Your everyday costume
is the life we wear

Here you are hidden, Love,
in plain sight

You stopped the game of hide and seek
and suddenly you were everywhere

This vision is the only priceless gem
in a rotting world

The mist of dreaming
can't withstand the dawn

Q & A

Q
What should I bring you?

A
Bring me an empty glass.
Bring me a broken shell.
Bring me a song set free.

Q
What is God's address?

A
If you ever find a place
where God does not exist,
do not build a house there.

Q

Why doesn't God wear a watch?

a

Because it's always now.

Q
In the darkness,
I can feel the light on my skin.
Can't I stay a little longer here in the dark,
so I can feel your light?

A
You fool, you are the light!
It is not outside of you.

Q
Which is better:
flower
fruit
seed
or
tree?

A
Whichever is now.
They are all filled with the same empty.

Q
These five horses
~touch, taste, hearing, smell, sight~
race toward illusion.

What is the horse that takes me to what is real?

A
It's a short trip.
You're already here.

Q
Will I always love you?

A
No, dear.
Soon there will be no "you"
only love.

Empty

This world has taught me many things
how to:
type and dance
work and play
argue and cook
pull weeds
paint pictures
dress in clothes
judge and be judged

how to be brave and tall
strong and vulnerable
loud and quiet
lovely and loveable
how to weep and be miserable
how to win

It taught me how to do business
this for that

But the world has not taught me
the one essential skill:
how to be nothing

I have a pile of concepts for sale
It'll cost you your life

You'll chase after pieces of paper
You'll believe you're a body
pretend it's not bound for dust
You'll believe that love is something limited
something outside
You'll believe that happiness can be bought
or bottled
You'll believe you exist

For the one who gives up all concepts
Life begins

My Master is so greedy
he takes and takes and takes

He took my loneliness, first
then my fear

He took my sorrow
and my pain

He took my tiredness
He took my lack
I think one day soon he'll even take "my"

Darkness flees before light
dissolves at its touch

Kindle the divine spark
and burn down the world

<u>Glass Half Full</u>

All this time I've been focused on the water
I should have been focused on the empty

The world says fill up
The Master says empty

The world says someday
Master says now

The world says play the game to win
Master says lose

The world says be somebody!
Master: be nothing

The world says dream a better dream
Master says wake up

And who my dear will you listen to?

The world says many many many many many
Master says only One

The world says love is just out there
Master says right here

And who my dear will you listen to?

Spill the water out
Leave me empty

Empty of thoughts
Empty of dreams
Empty of wishes
Empty of need
Empty of want

This empty is the most fulfilled I have ever felt

This not knowing, not being
is the sweetest of all

My atoms
are dancing
in your empty

You told me to leave
What was left was you

Without the distorting lens of the ego
everything is pulsing energy, bliss

Isn't this love?
you asked

It must be, but I don't recognize it
without an object

If feels alive
It feels awake

It is not bravery to battle
It is bravery to let go

The caterpillar wants just one more cabbage leaf
but the butterfly can't wait to be born

Drop it!
and dissolve

On the dance floor

There is no past mistake
There is no prior success

There is only the present moment
and how alive you want to be in it

NOW is too tiny to fit identities
and too vast for limitation

You cannot sail across it
to the past
or to the future

In countless universes
it is the only thing that is real

It is the doorway to the infinite
The only place where I can meet you

Line by line the ink runs from the pages
the glue cracks and peels away
the binding comes unfastened

Page by page
the story is unwritten

It's time to burn
the Book of Me

In the school of the Beloved
learn to drink the water you're in

Learn to be breathed by the kiss of the Lover

Learn to let go of temporary things

Thread by thread
learn to become unwoven
and unbound

I saw you
and the door to the Beloved opened wide

By the time you came knocking
there were no walls on the house

Flight

The door to the Beloved
isn't always open

But you can slip through the keyhole
if you are carrying nothing

When I saw a bird's nest on the ground
I thought it was a tragedy

Until I realized it was summer
and the bird had flown

The ego cries
looking down at the earth it lost below . . .
getting farther away

It forgot to look up
to see that we are soaring

In the moment of leaping
something in me cries out for solid ground

The soul shakes like a wet dog
saying: leave it all behind

The Choice

I could try to bind myself
back to the giant weight
the Beloved just freed me from
Embrace it with both arms, hold on,
and wait for it to embrace me back

I could walk away and be free
Maybe find another stone to sit on

Or just not be

If there are one or one thousand
flowers in the garden
the sun shines the same
Don't blame the sun if you decide not to bloom

On a desert or a lake the rain drops down
Don't blame the clouds if you don't drink it in

The ocean is thousands of miles wide
Don't blame the ocean if you don't jump in

The sky wraps a circle
all the way around the earth
Don't blame the sky if you decide not to fly

Sweep me up in your infinity
I'll drop everything I don't have

Sweep me up in your infinity
I am only yours

Swept up in your Love
Like a drop in the ocean wave

Like a spark in an explosion
Swept away

Like a word in a poem
Like breath in a gasp

Like a dancer in the dance
Swept away

Like a lover in the Love
Swept away

I am feasting on Love
Light drips from these drunk lips

I sleep so that you can wake me
Stand close so you can embrace me
I'm always hanging around the hive

I walk the hallways of my childhood
armed with a new grace

Grace floods the fires of torment
sets fire to the brittle fears

One thread at a time
the endless woven patterns come unraveled

When there are no more
of these hallways to walk on
Flight

Delicious freedom from the chains of
"this is me"

I had to break the vase of love
to let the Love out

As long as you were worshipping clay
the nectar couldn't flow

I had to kill your cows
or you would still be tending to them
and not embracing the sky

You can hold the pieces and cry
for all those lost illusions
Or you can open your eyes
to what you seek:

A Love beyond boundaries
A Love beyond caretaking
A Love beyond the vulnerable child
A Love beyond waking

On the other side of the prison door
is not another cell
another vase
another cow
It is a world without walls
Light

Somewhere between a lover's euphoria
and falling awake
the dark velvet hand of meditation embraces

The touch of the Lover
claims me
bathes me
lifts me
washes me with light so there is nothing

The heart thrills
the mind dissolves
there is nothing

The heart trills
floating
nothing

I had plans
before you erased me

Dizzy
with the
weightless
end of slavery

I bloom
and the word
blooms with me

Through the open spaces
where walls once stood
a shower of flower petals
line the path
of not-me

The touch of the Lover cannot be described
Yet still I sing

About the Author

Adria Estribou is a freelance writer and editor in Hawaii. She is in her third decade of meditation, this time around. She delights in words almost as much as she loves silence.

Drop her a line, drink from the drunk poet blog, or keep up to date with new releases at www.adriaestribou.com.